To _____

From _____

MY FAVORITE RECIPE:

Signed _____   _____

Date _____   _____

Famous Florida! ® Key Lime Cookin'
Famous Recipes from Famous Places™

For information address:
Seaside Publishing, Post Office Box 14441
St.Petersburg, Florida 33733

Seaside Books may be purchased for educational, sales, or business promotional use. For information please write:

Seaside Publishing
Special Markets Department,
Post Office Box 14441, St. Petersburg, Florida 33733
Toll Free Order Line: *888-FLA-BOOK (800-352-2665)*

Seaside Publishing
A Division of Famous Florida! ® Enterprises, Inc.
ISBN: 0-942084-30-6
Library of Congress Catalog No: 87-063166

Cover Design by Peggy Herring

Send comments and suggestions to:
Seaside Publishing
Attention: Editors
P.O. Box 14441
St. Petersburg, FL 33733

Order our books and Certified Key Lime Juice Online at: famousflorida.com

INTRODUCTION: THE "KEY" INGREDIENT

Since the last quarter of the 1800s, tourism has been a major industry and the number one money crop for our Sunshine State. Sun-seekers flock to Florida to bask in our glorious sun, fish in our turquoise-tinted waters, and frolic in our vast array of magical attractions.

Florida.... we love it! It's a picture- postcard of swaying palms and beautiful turquoise waters, a boomtown paradise covered with condos and glorious mansions, neon flamingos and visitors flocking into the land of Mickey and Minnie, with an occasional visitor asking, "Which way to the islands?"

A veritable "fountain of youth" to many a newcomer to our state, Florida has always been a magnet for drawing people seeking their fondest dreams and desires. Always striving for growth and development, at times our precious state has tried to provide visitors and residents alike with a bounty of unforgettable treasures, including some of the best Key Lime pie and you'll ever taste.

But, wait a minute, how does one not familiar with the precious juice know if they are tasting the real thing? Here's a few hints: Read the label on the Key Lime juice you purchase. It should say "Key Lime" juice. Note the taste of the juice; it's different from the typical juice we most often purchase.   *(over)*

Remember this; the flavor is like no other. It's very tart in comparison with regular lime juice, a "one-of-a-kind" flavor. Once you've had it, there is absolutely no comparison with the more ubiquitous limes. For fun, you may want to do a "taste test" and compare.

Once you taste, I know you'll agree that we're not talking about any ordinary run-of the mill lime, but about a precious, fragile, tart-like one-of-a-kind flavor - one which lingers long after the meal is over.

The infamous Key Lime pie is said to have originated in the alluring and mysterious Florida Keys and the cause of national "erotomania" for the tiny ovid precious little fruit. Ahhhhh-inspiring, to say the least.

Truly Tropical!

What about this diminutive fruit, what's <u>so</u> different about it?

Our research shows that Key Lime, also known as the Mexican or West Indian lime, is the only truly tropical species of citrus. It biological name, citrus aurantifolia, comes from the latin words for "gold" and "leaf."

The Key Lime is a thin-skinned, almost round or ellipsoid fruit, about 1-1/2 to 2-1/4 inches long, and is usually picked while still green. The white flowers are fragrant and very beautiful, with branches densely armed with short stiff spines.

When the fruit is cut open, its pulp reveals a greenish-yellow coloring. Each fruit is divided into about ten sections enclosing rice-like cells that contain a sour juice of high citric acid content rich in mineral potassium. "True" Key Lime juice is never green, although many a restaurateur (here in Florida, and elsewhere) has been known to add green food coloring to his pie.

The Tree of Life

The fragrantly oily fruit matures about five months after the blooms appear, and bearing begins in the third or fourth year from setting. Young trees and those well-cared for on good soil can produce upwards of 125 barrels or more per acre per year! When fully ripe, the luscious fruit is bright yellow and very fragrant. For shipping fruits must be picked while still green, since ripe ones bruise very easily. Shipping the fruit is difficult because of their innate fragility.

SPECIAL KITCHEN HINTS

The juice of three Key Limes is equal to that of one of our commercially sold limes which are called Persian, or Tahitian limes. From one of these "common" limes you can extract 1-2 tablespoons of lime juice, depending on the juiciness of the fruit, which will vary. In the much smaller Key Lime you can expect to extract 1 to 2 teaspoons of juice per fruit. One-quarter cup of juice measures exactly 4 tablespoons of juice.

If you're unable to get fresh limes, use my bottled real Key Lime juice, <u>Famous Florida! Key Lime Juice</u>. But be sure to check the label to make certain it's the real thing! My bottles say "Key Lime" juice, not just "lime" juice. And remember, just because it's from Key West does not mean it's <u>real</u> Key Lime Juice. In Florida, much of the bottled lime juice is made from Persian (or Tahitian) limes, not the real "key" ingredient.

The shelf life of a bottle of our Key lime juice is approximately 12 months. Once opened, tighten the cap and keep refrigerated. If your juice turns brown, it's time to toss. For best results, keep your juice away from direct sunlight and heat.

I've included recipes in this new revised collection from my original 1986 book, "The Key Lime Cookbook", (from true Conchs - native residents of the Keys), as well as new recipes from Florida and Caribbean restaurants, along with many of my own. I have paid heed to the latest guidelines for health. Be assured these recipes are healthful, as well as delicious.

I trust that you will truly become as "addicted" as I have to the wonderful, exotic Key Lime. I'm pleased to share these very special recipes with you.

Tropically Yours,

Joyce LaFray

Key Lime Cookin'

by
Joyce LaFray

KEY CONTENTS:

POULTRY:

Island Seasoned Chicken, 37
Barbecued Chicken, 38
Cuban Key Lime Chicken, 39
Key Lime Curry Chicken, 40
Key West Chicken Broil, 42
Veal Key West, 43

SAUCES AND CONDIMENTS:

Old Sour, 45
Hot Cocktail Sauce, 46
Keys Mustard Sauce, 47
Key Lime Raisin Sauce, 48

PIES, PIES AND MORE KEY LIME PIES:

Pier House Key Lime Pie, 49
Joe's Stone Crab Key Lime Pie, 51
Classic Key Lime Pie, 52
Key Lime Rainbow, 53
Kooky Key Lime Pie, 55
Cross Creek Key Lime Pie, 56
Eggless Key Lime Pie, 57
Whipped Chocolate Key Lime Pie, 58
Meringue Key Lime Pie, 59
Mile High Key Lime Pie, 61
Captiva Key Lime Pie, 62

OTHER DECADENT DESSERTS:

No Bake Cheesecake, 63
Low-Cal Key Lime Delight, 64
Key Lime Butternut Cookies, 65
Pillow Cake, 66
Aunt Betty's Key Lime Cake, 69
Deep Dish Sabayon Tart, 70
Key Lime Sherbert, 71
Citrus Sorbet, 72
Frozen Whipped Delight, 73
Key West Slices, 74
Miami Key Lime Spiced Mangoes, 75
Key Lime Bread, 76

Key West Limeade

1 cup Key Lime juice
3/4 cup granulated sugar, or honey to taste
4 cups (1 quart) fresh tap or bottled water
Cracked ice to fill glasses
Fresh mint sprigs
Maraschino cherries

Add granulated sugar to Key Lime juice and blend well. Add water, and cracked ice and mix well. Pour into glasses.

Garnish with mint sprigs and maraschino cherries.

Serves: 4

Key Lime Cooler

4 cups cold sparkling bottled water, such as San
  Pellegrino*
3/4 cup granulated sugar, or sugar substitute
Juice of 15 Key Limes
2 cups white grape juice
4 slices Key Lime
Mint sprigs for garnish

       Place water into a large pitcher. Add sugar,
or sugar substitute, then add grape and Key Lime
juice. Stir well with long handled wooden spoon.
Pour into tall cooler glasses filled with crushed ice.
       Garnish with fresh mint sprigs and Key Lime
slices.

*Any sparkling water may be substituted.

Makes: About 1 1/4 quarts

Big Pine Key Lime Cocktail

Juice of 2 Key Limes
3/4 ounces apricot brandy
1 1/2 ounces white* rum
Crushed ice
Slice of Key Lime
Maraschino cherry for garnish

Combine all ingredients with crushed ice in a cocktail shaker. Strain into a chilled 10-ounce cocktail glass.

Garnish with Key Lime and maraschino cherry.

*For an extra punch, use overproof rum (151 proof)!

Serves: 1

Cuban Special

Juice of 3 Key Limes
1 tablespoon pineapple juice
1 ounce white or golden rum
1 teaspoon Triple Sec liqueur
1 cup cracked ice
Peel of Key Lime for garnish
Maraschino cherry for garnish

Combine all ingredients in a shaker. Add ice.
Shake well until ice cold, then strain into a cocktail
glass. Garnish with Key Lime peel and a cherry.

Serves: 1

Mojito*

1 teaspoon granulated sugar
Juice of 3 Key Limes
2 sprigs mint
1 1/2 ounces white rum
Cracked ice
Soda water

     Place 1 mint sprig, Key Lime juices and granulated sugar into a 10-ounce glass. Blend with a long spoon crushing leaves to extract juice. Add white rum, then soda water to top. Stir well. Add second sprig of mint. Stir again. Serve with a straw

*This recipe is the authentic classic favorite of Cubans.

Serves: 1

Frozen Key Lime Margarita

3 tablespoons Key Lime juice
1 cup Tequila*
5 tablespoons Cointreau
4-5 cups crushed ice
Margarita salt to frost rim of glasses
Key Lime slices for garnish

Dip rim of Margarita glass in a little Key Lime juice, then dip into a plate of Margarita salt and allow a few seconds to dry.

In the container of a blender combine Key Lime juice, Tequila, and Cointreau. Blend on low speed for a few seconds, then add the crushed ice and turn to high speed and process until frozen drink consistency. Do not over process.

Pour into prepared Margarita cocktail glasses and garnish each with a Key Lime slice.

*For an extra punch, use Tequilla gold liquor.

Serves: 4

Key Lime Mai Tai

8 ounces (1 cup) white rum
4 ounces (1/2 cup) Key Lime juice
2 ounces almond syrup
1/4 cup granulated sugar, or honey
8 ounces (1 cup) fresh orange juice
1 ounce fresh grapefruit juice
4 dashes grenadine syrup
4 cups cracked ice
4 Key Lime slices
4 orange slices
4 maraschino cherries

    Place all ingredients in the container of a blender or food processor. Process for a few seconds, then pour over cracked ice packed into tall cooler glasses.
    Garnish each glass with a Key Lime slice, orange slice and a maraschino cherry.

Serves: 4

Original Daiquiri*

Cracked ice
3 ounces white rum
1/2 ounce Key Lime juice
1 teaspoon granulated sugar
Slice of Key Lime or lemon for garnish

Fill a cocktail shaker with cracked ice. Add rum, fresh lime juice and sugar. Shake well and strain into a chilled cocktail glass.

Garnish with a slice of Key Lime that has been cut halfway through so it can be attached to the rim of the glass.

*While the cocktail is a purely American drink, the daiquiri cocktail was named after the Daiquiri Iron Mines near Santiago, Cuba in the late 1890's.

Serves: 1

Stone Crab With Pier House Mustard Sauce

1 quart mayonnaise
1 cup dark brown mustard, such as Gulden's
1 cup Key Lime juice
4-6 pounds Stone Crabs*, chilled
Key Limes or lime wedges

     To prepare the sauce for the stone crabs, whisk mustard and mayonnaise together in a medium size glass bowl. Slowly pour in the Key Lime juice and whisk until sauce is smooth. Chill for about 1/2 hour or more.
     Serve sauce in small ramekins with chilled mustard sauce, along with drawn butter and Key Lime wedges.

*Since most harvested stone crabs are frozen immediately after being caught, this savory shellfish is purchased already cooked. If frozen, defrost before serving.

serves: 4

Fresh Key Lime Salsa

4 medium very ripe tomatoes, peeled, seeded and
  diced
1 fresh jalapeno pepper*, seeded and minced
1 tablespoon chopped fresh cilantro leaves
1 medium red onion, minced
1/2 teaspoon granulated sugar
1/2 teaspoon salt, or to taste
1/2 teaspoon freshly ground black pepper, or to
taste
Juice of 2 Key Limes

　　　　In a medium size glass bowl mix together the
tomatoes, jalapeno pepper, cilantro, onion, sugar,
and salt and pepper. Combine well. Add in the juice,
cover and refrigerate for 4-5 hours before serving.

Serve with fresh tortilla chips.

*You may substitute any similarly hot pepper.

Serves: 4

Key Lime Avocado Dip

2 large ripe avocadoes, peeled
3 tablespoons Key Lime juice
1 teaspoon ground chili pepper
2 dashes Tabasco, or other hot sauce
1/2 teaspoon salt, or to taste
1 tablespoon minced sweet red onion
1 ripe tomato, diced

Allow time to prepare this recipe about one hour before serving. Mash avocadoes well by hand, or mash in the container of a food processor, but do not puree; you want somewhat of a chunky consistency. Add remaining ingredients and blend well. Refrigerate.

Serve with freshly fried tortilla chips or store bought chips.

Serves: 4-6

Joyce's Key West Conch Dip

1 cup conch*, finely ground
1 8-ounce package cream cheese
1 tablespoon milk
1 tablespoon Key Lime juice
1/2 teaspoon Worcestershire sauce
2 cloves fresh garlic, peeled and finely chopped
1 tablespoon sweet red onion, finely chopped
1 tablespoon finely chopped red pepper
1 tablespoon finely chopped green pepper
Dash of Tabasco sauce, or other hot pepper sauce
Salt and coarsely ground black pepper to taste
Paprika for garnish

    Blend the cream cheese by hand or with a food processor with the milk until smooth. Add in Key Lime juice and Worcestershire and continue to blend until smooth. Mix in the garlic, onion, red and green bell pepper, Tabasco sauce and salt and black pepper to taste. Garnish with paprika.
    Serve with fresh tortilla chips or vegetable crudites.

*To tenderize conch, beat conch with a heavy mallet, then add to food processor and process until finely ground.

Serves: 4-6

Pier House Conch Seviche

1 pound raw conch, chopped*
2/3 cup Key Lime juice
1 cucumber, finely chopped
1/2 red onion, seeded and finely chopped
1/2 fresh jalapeno pepper, finely chopped
1/4 red bell pepper, seeded and finely chopped
2 tablespoons chopped parsley, finely chopped
1/4 cup vegetable oil, or other oil
3 cups coconut milk**
Dash Tabasco
1 tablespoon granulated sugar
1/2 teaspoon salt, or to taste
Dash coarsely ground black pepper
Leafy lettuce
Red Bermuda onion, thinly sliced
Cucumber and fresh basil leaves for garnish
Edible flowers (optional)

One day ahead grind fresh or defrosted conch, and place in a large glass bowl. Add in Key Lime juice, mix well, then cover and allow to marinate in refrigerator for 24 hours. The lime juice will "cook" the conch. When marinated, drain off excess liquid and discard. Add to the bowl with the marinated conch, the oil, coconut milk, tabasco, sugar, salt, and black pepper. Combine well and adjust seasonings to suit taste.

(continued)

Serve seviche on a bed of lettuce decorated with thin sliced bermuda onion, sprouts, cucumber and basil. Garnish with fresh edible flowers.

* To tenderize conch properly, beat with a heavy mallet, then add to food processor and process until pieces are about a 1/4" dice.

**You can purchase canned coconut milk at most supermarkets, or make your own.

Serves: 6

Scallop Seviche

2 cups fresh bay scallops
1/3 cup Key Lime juice or lime juice
1/3 cup green bell peppers
1/3 cup red bell peppers
1/3 cup yellow peppers, finely diced
2 scallions, trimmed and diced
1 ripe tomato, diced
1 teaspoon chopped fresh dill
Salt and white pepper to taste

Place all ingredients in a large bowl and softly fold. Marinate refrigerated for about 1 hour. Serve on bed of leafy greens.

Serves: 4

Seafood Cocktail With Key Lime Sauce

2 tablespoons prepared horseradish
1/3 cup ketchup
2 tablespoons chili sauce
1/4 cup tablespoons Key Lime juice
1 teaspoon Louisiana hot sauce

    Mix all ingredients together thoroughly. Chill. Pour over assorted fresh seafood such as clams, oysters, shrimp, crabmeat and shelled lobster.

Makes: About 1 cup sauce
Serves: 4

Tropical Salad

1/2 teaspoon kosher salt
1/2 teaspoon Dijon mustard
1/4 cup Key Lime juice
1/2 cup extra virgin olive oil
1 teaspoon granulated sugar
2 heads bibb lettuce

Add ingredients to the container of a food processor or blender. Process well for about 6-8 seconds.

Use sparingly on bibb lettuce, leafy greens or freshly blanched asparagus, green beans or haricot verts.

Makes: About 3/4 cup dressing
Serves: 4

Bahama Mama Key Lime Conch Salad

3 medium size conchs*
1 cup celery, peeled and diced
1 cup sweet onion, diced
1 green bell pepper, seeded and diced
1 tablespoon red bell pepper, seeded and diced
1 large ripe tomato, seeded and diced
Juice of 1 sour orange
Juice of 6 Key Limes
1 cucumber, peeled and chopped
1/2 teaspoon Tabasco or other hot pepper sauce
2 Key Limes, cut into fourths for garnish

Tenderize the conch pieces by beating with a heavy metal or wooden mallet for about 5-10 minutes on the membrane side of the conch. Cut each into a 1/4" dice and place in a medium size glass bowl. Add the orange and lime juice and combine well. Allow to marinate overnight.

In a separate small bowl, combine the diced celery, onion, green pepper, tomato and cucumber, then add to the marinated conch mixture. Mix well, then season with hot pepper sauce. Chill.

Serve in a chilled glass bowl with Key Lime wedges and orange wedges for garnish.

*It is of utmost importance that conch be well-tenderized so that it will not be tough. Conch may be purchased from most seafood markets frozen in 5 pound boxes.

Serves: 1 as an entree, 2 as an appetizer

Key West Avocado Salad

4 conch, tenderized* and finely chopped
1 sweet white onion, finely chopped
1 red bell pepper, seeded and finely chopped
3 tablespoons Key Lime juice
1 teaspoon fresh cilantro
1 teaspoon fresh parsley
1 teaspoon fresh thyme
1/2 cup extra virgin** olive oil
1 tablespoon white vinegar
1 teaspoon Jamaican curry powder, or other medium
 curry powder
2 tablespoons Old Sour (see page —)
 Salt and coarsely ground black pepper to taste
2 avocadoes, halved and seeded
1 head Bibb lettuce, or other soft lettuce
 Fresh chopped parsley for garnish
 Paprika for garnish

In a medium size glass bowl, combine the tenderized marinated conch with the onion, red bell pepper, Key Lime juice, cilantro, parsley, thyme, extra virgin olive oil, vinegar, curry powder, Old Sour, salt and coarsely ground black pepper. Cover and marinate refrigerated overnight or at least 8 hours.

(continued)

When ready to serve, check seasoning, place two avocado halves on a leafy bed of lettuce, then spoon the marinated conch mixture into the halved avocadoes.

Sprinkle with paprika and fresh chopped parsley for garnish.

*To tenderize conch, beat conch with a heavy mallet, then add to food processor and process until finely ground.

**You may use regular olive oil for this salad, but the extra virgin, which is the first press of the olives has a more intense and exciting flavor.

Serves: 2

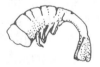

Caicos Conch Salad

6 medium conch, cleaned and tenderized
Juice of 2 sour oranges*, or regular oranges
Juice of 12 Key Limes
4 stalks celery, peeled and finely chopped
2 white onions, chopped
2 green bell peppers, seeded and chopped
2 large ripe tomatoes, seeded and chopped
2 cucumbers, peeled and diced
Tabasco sauce, or other hot pepper sauce to taste
2 Key Limes cut into wedges for garnish

Tenderize the conch by beating with a heavy metal or wooden mallet for 5-10 minutes. Chop conch into small 1/4" pieces, then, cover, add sour orange or orange juice and Key Lime juice and combine well. Cover and marinate refrigerated overnight, or for
at least 8 hours.

When marinated, combine the celery, onion, green pepper, tomato and cucumber, then add to the marinated conch and mix well. Season with Tabasco sauce and salt and pepper to taste.

Chill and serve in a chilled glass bowl with wedges of Key Lime for garnish.

*Sour oranges are available in many tropical areas and often used to marinate conch. The juice imparts a more tart flavor to the salad. Any other fresh orange juice may be substituted for a similar flavor.

Serves: 4

Mesclun of Greens With Key Lime Dressing

Salad Dressing:
1 clove garlic, chopped
1/2 cup extra virgin* olive oil
1/4 cup Key Lime juice
2 tablespoon honey
2 tablespoons chopped sweet red onion
  Salt and cracked pepper to taste

Greens & Garnish:
4 cups mixed salad greens (bibb, red leaf,
  arugula,etc.)
1/2 cup chopped pistachio nuts
1 cup fresh Valencia oranges, seeded, sliced,
  membrane removed
4 sprigs fresh mint leaves, chopped
1 cup Key Lime Honey Dressing

  Place all salad dressing ingredients in the container of a blender or food processor. Process for a 4-5 seconds until all ingredients are well emulsified. Set aside.
  Prepare greens by placing 1 cup of the mixed greens on each of 4 large chilled salad plates. Lace each plate with 2-3 ounces of the Key Lime dressing. Garnish with pistachios, oranges and mint leaves.

*You may use any kind of oil, but extra virgin, the first press of the olives has a more "exciting" flavor than most.

Serves: 4

Key Lime Honey Fruit Salad

1/4 cup granulated sugar
  Juice of 1 dozen Key Limes (About 1 cup juice)
1 cup pineapple juice
1/2 cup honey
2 ounces Grand Marnier or Amaretto liqueur
4 oranges, halved, with shells reserved
1 pink or yellow grapefruit, peeled, pith removed and sectioned
1 ripe pineapple, peeled and diced
1/2 pound seedless red grapes, halved
1 very ripe mango, peeled, seeded and diced
1/4 teaspoon celery seeds
Escarole, endive or other leafy greens

     Add to a medium saucepan the Key Lime juice, pineapple juice and celery seeds. Bring to a boil. Add in the honey, liqueur and combine well with the oranges, grapefruit, pineapple, grapes and mango. Spoon salad into reserved orange shells.
     Place one or two filled shells on a bed of leafy greens and place a seeded grape in the center of each.

Serves: 4 - 8

Key's Steamed Shrimp

10-12 Key Limes, thinly sliced
3 sprigs fresh dill sprigs
3 bay leaves
3 whole cloves garlic, peeled
3 sprigs fresh parsley
2 sprigs fresh thyme
1 tablespoon whole black peppercorns
2 carrots, thinly sliced
2 onions, thinly sliced
2 cups dry white wine such, as Chardonnay
3 cups fish stock, clam broth, or water
3 pound medium size shrimp, shells on
1 stick (1/4 pound) sweet unsalted butter, melted

Combine all ingredients except wine, fish stock and shrimp in the bottom of a fish poacher or large steamer. Pour in the wine and fish stock. Simmer for about 25 minutes, then add in the shrimp and cook until shrimp turns translucent. Do not overcoook.

Drain shrimp and serve piping hot with drawn butter, or cocktail sauce if you prefer.

Serves: 6

Key Lime Grouper With Fresh Herbs

3 tablespoons olive oil
4-6 ounce portions grouper*
2 tablespoon Key Lime juice
1 tablespoon chopped shallots, or white onion
1 teaspoon fresh tarragon
1/2 teaspoon fresh chives
3 Key Limes, thinly sliced
1/2 teaspoon cayenne pepper
1/2 cup chopped red bell pepper
Salt and coarsely ground black pepper to taste

Preheat oven to 325 degrees F.

Pour olive oil into a shallow pyrex baking dish. Place fillets in pan and then turn several times to coat well. Drizzle Key Lime juice over all and turn again.

In a separate small bowl combine shallots, tarragon, chives, cayenne pepper. Sprinkle evenly over fillets.

Cover loosely with foil and bake for about 10-12 minutes, or until fish is just done. Do not overcook.

Remove from oven, pour juices over all and serve garnished with Key Lime wedges and chopped red bell pepper.

*Any firm white fish can be substituted.

Serves: 4

Key Lime Baked Snapper

1 1/2 pounds red snapper fillets, or other firm
  white fish
2 tablespoons Key Lime juice
1 tablespoon melted butter
1 1/2 teaspoons grated lime peel
Salt* and coarsely ground pepper to taste
Pinch of nutmeg
Fresh chopped parsley for garnish
Fresh Key Lime wedges for garnish

Preheat oven to 350 degrees F. Cut snapper fillets into 6 serving-size pieces.

Combine the Key Lime juice, butter, Key Lime peel, black pepper and nutmeg. Mix thoroughly, then spoon over fish to cover completely. Bake uncovered, basting with pan juices until the fish flakes easily, about 15 minutes or even less for very thin fillets.

Garnish fish with fresh parsley sprigs and lime wedges.

*Use sea salt on seafood when possible; it will further enhance the flavor.

Serves: 4

Big Pine Broiled Fillets

2 pounds fresh firm fish fillets, such as
red snapper or grouper
1/4 cup Key Lime Juice
3 tablespoons melted butter, or margarine
Sea salt and cracked pepper to taste
1/2 teaspoon thyme
1/2 teaspoon rosemary, crushed
1/2 teaspoon paprika
1/2 cup butter, or margarine melted
1 tablespoon fresh parsley

Set oven to broil, or prepare indoor or
outdoor grill.

Place fresh fillets in a shallow baking pan and
sprinkle on Key Lime juice. Turn fillets to coat well,
then place dots of butter on top of each fillet, or a
sprinkling of olive oil on each. Season with sea salt,
black pepper, thyme and rosemary, so that all
pieces are coated. Sprinkle paprika on top of each.
Broil until fish turns white and flakes.

Melt the butter or margarine, then mix with
fresh parsley and serve on side as sauce.

Serves: 4

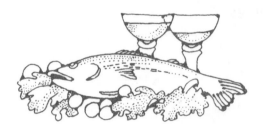

Fresh Trout With Key Lime Butter

4 8-10 ounce servings whole trout*, cleaned and
  dressed
Salt and cracked pepper to taste
1/2 teaspoon cayenne pepper
1 teaspoon Worcestershire Sauce
1/2 cup Key Lime juice
1 cup all-purpose flour
1/4 cup melted butter or margarine
Juice of 3 Key Limes
1/2 cup slivered and toasted almonds
1 tablespoon chopped fresh parsley for garnish
3 Key Limes, thinly sliced for garnish

Season each fish with salt, cracked pepper
and cayenne to taste. Dip each piece into the flour
and coat well on both sides.

Heat a large skillet, then add butter or
margarine, and when butter is heated add 2 of the
fillets. Cook on each side for about 4-5 minutes,
until completely cooked through, turning gently.
Repeat for the remaining 2 fillets.

Place fish on a heated plate, reserving pan
drippings. Add in Key Lime juice and bring to a boil.
Place 1/4 of the almonds over each portion, then
pour pan drippings over each and sprinkle with
parsley. Garnish with Key Lime slices.

*This recipe can also be used for most other types of whole fish or
fillets.

Serves: 4

Grilled Pompano
Key Lime

1/2 cup Key Lime juice
4 6-ounce pompano filets, or other firm white fish
2 cups milk
8 tablespoons olive oil
1 tablespoon chopped garlic
1 red bell pepper, minced
1 pound medium size shrimp, peeled and deveined
1 1/3 cups pureed roasted yellow pepper
Chopped parsley for garnish
Mango chutney relish* (optional)

Soak fillets for 1/2 hour in milk to remove any "fishy" odor. Sprinkle each pompano with Key Lime juice, then brush each pompano fillet with one tablespoon of olive oil. Grill over medium-hot coals for two minutes on each side, turning carefully so not to break fillet. Remove to low oven to keep warm.

In a 10-12 inch skillet over medium-high heat, heat remaining olive oil. When oil is heated and begins to smell fragrant, add garlic, red bell pepper and shrimp. Saute' about two minutes or until shrimp turns white and is done.

Using a large serving spoon, place one fillet on each plate with a portion of the yellow pureed pepper around each. Garnish with freshly chopped parsley.

Serve with mango chutney relish on the side.

*May be purchased on most supermarkets.

Serves: 4

Island Seasoned Chicken

1 3-4 pound frying chicken, cut into small pieces
1/2 cup Key Lime juice
1/3 cup soy sauce
4 garlic cloves, finely chopped
4 tablespoons olive oil
2 white onions, diced
Salt and coarsely cracked black pepper to taste.

     Wash the chicken pieces in cold water, dry with paper towels, then rub skin with 1 garlic clove. Mix together the Key Lime juice, soy sauce and the remaining garlic cloves. Marinate refrigerated overnight, or at least 8 hours.
     Heat a 10-12" frying pan, and when heated add the olive oil. When oil begins to smell fragrant add the chicken pieces. Season well with salt and pepper. Brown on both sides over high heat, turning several times. When browned reduce heat, then add onions and remaining marinade. Bring to a boil, cover and simmer for about an hour, or until done.

Serves: 4

Barbecued Chicken

2 3-4 pound whole chickens, cut in half for
   barbecuing
3 Key Limes, rinds grated
1 tablespoon unsalted butter or margarine
1 medium onion, finely chopped
3 large cloves garlic, minced
1-2/3 cups ketchup
1/4 cup balsamic vinegar
1/3 cup honey
3 tablespoons Worcestershire sauce
1 tablespoon Pickapeppa sauce
1 tablespoon dark brown mustard
Salt and coarsely ground pepper to taste.

Slice the Key Limes (grate rind and set
aside) in half, squeeze the juice into a small bowl
and set aside.

In a medium-sized saucepan, melt the butter
or margarine and saute' the onion until translucent,
for about 2-3 minutes. Add the lime rind and garlic
and saute' and stir for about 2 minutes, then add
lime juice and rind and remaining ingredients.
Combine together well. Bring to a boil, reduce heat,
and simmer for about 20-25 minutes. Season to
taste.

Wash and rub dry chickens before marinating.
Add chicken pieces to 3/4's of the sauce, cover
and marinate refrigerated for 2-3 hours before
barbecuing. Baste with sauce while barbecuing and
serve remaining sauce on the side. Season to taste
with salt and pepper.

Serves: 4-6 persons

Cuban Key Lime Chicken

4 - 4 1/2 pounds chicken pieces, skin removed
3 cloves garlic, peeled and crushed
1 teaspoon ground cumin
1 lemon, sliced with seeds removed
1/4 cup fresh Key Lime juice
1/4 cup orange juice
1 cup thinly sliced white onion
1/4 cup olive oil for frying
1 3-ounce jar pimiento pieces
1 teaspoon coarsely ground black pepper
Salt to taste

Wash and pat dry chicken pieces with paper towels. Set aside.

Mix together garlic, cumin and lemon slices, lime and orange juice, then pour over chicken pieces. Cover pieces with onion rings and marinate for about 3 hours, or longer.

Saute' chicken slices in olive oil until golden brown. Add pimiento, then season with salt and pepper. Add marinaded ingredients. Cook over medium high heat for about 5 minutes, then turn to simmer and cook for another 25-30 minutes, or until done.

Serves: 6-8

Key Lime Curry Chicken

1 large chicken breast, diced
Salt to taste
1/2 cup Key Lime juice
3 cloves fresh garlic, finely chopped
2 tablespoons medium - hot curry powder
2 tablespoons olive oil, or unsalted butter
1 white onion, finely chopped
1 green bell pepper, seeded and finely chopped
1/2 cup chopped very ripe tomatoes
1 tablespoon peeled and diced celery
1 teaspoon coarsely ground black pepper
1 cup water
1-2 tablespoons cornstarch
White jasmine rice, or other white rice
Curry condiments:
1/2 - 1 cup of the following condiments:
mango chutney, coconut, scallions, very ripe seeded
tomatoes and chopped unsalted peanuts.

Wash and pat chicken pieces dry. Season with
fresh Key Lime juice by briskly rinsing first with
water, then with the lime juice.

(continued)

40

Saute' garlic and curry powder, stirring constantly, in the olive oil for a few minutes, then add onion, green pepper, tomatoes, celery, and ground pepper. Saute' until the vegetables are done. Add about 1 cup of water to the mixture and mix gently. Mix the cornstarch with a little water to make a paste then add to the mixture, adding enough to make a
medium thick sauce. Add in the chicken pieces and cook until done, time but do not overcook. Adjust seasoning.

Serve with a selection of curry condiments in small bowls or lazy susan. Serve with fluffy brown rice.

Serves: 4

Key West Chicken Broil

2 pound boned chicken breasts,* sliced into 2" x 1" pieces
2 tablespoons honey
1 tablespoon water
2 garlic cloves, finely chopped
1/2 teaspoon salt
1/2 teaspoon coarsely cracked black pepper
1/2 teaspoon ground red hot pepper flakes
1/2 teaspoon basil
2 cups cooked white or brown rice

Preheat oven to 425 degrees F.

Mix honey with water to thin. In a large glass bowl combine honey with all other ingredients except chicken. Add in chicken pieces and coat well so that all pieces are covered, then bake for about 25 minutes, or until pieces are thoroughly cooked, but be careful not to overcook.

Remove pieces to broiler coated with aluminum foil. Broil until golden brown for about 3-4 minutes.

Garnish with fresh chopped parsley and serve over white or brown rice with a leafy green salad.

*This recipe can also be done with any selection of chicken pieces.

Serves: 4

Veal Key West

12 2-ounce pieces veal scaloppine*
1 cup all-purpose flour
3 tablespoons butter or margarine
1 teaspoon Key Lime juice
1/2 cup dry white wine
4 shallots, finely minced
3/4 pound fresh wild** mushrooms, thinly sliced
3/4 teaspoon fresh chopped Italian parsley
Salt and coarsely ground black pepper to taste
1 - ounce brandy
1 pound cooked fettuccine or other egg noodles
Key Lime or lime wedges for garnish

    Dredge scaloppine pieces lightly in flour. In a large saute' pan, melt the butter or margarine and brown scallops over medium heat turning at least once, until completely cooked. Using a slotted spoon, remove scallops from the pan and set aside.

    Add the shallots and mushrooms to the pan with the drippings and cook for 4-5 minutes, being carefully not to burn. Add in the Key Lime juice and wine and cook for 1-2 minutes longer. Add back the reserved veal pieces back to the pan and cook for about 2-3 minutes.

(continued)

Pour brandy over the top of veal pieces and flambe.

Serve over fresh cooked noodles and garnish with chopped parsley and Key Lime or lime wedges.

* You can prepare your own scaloppine by pounding veal thinly between waxed paper and cutting into small pieces, or your butcher may do it for you.

**You may use regular mushrooms, but the flavor of wild mushrooms greatly enhances the dish.

Serves: 4

Old Sour

2 cups Key Lime juice
2 teaspoons salt
4 whole hot bird peppers,* or several drops of hot
sauce or cayenne to taste

Add salt and hot peppers or hot pepper sauce
to the Key Lime juice. Cover loosely and let stand at
room temperature for one or two days.
Strain the Key Lime juice through a piece of
cheesecloth until the liquid is clear and free of
fragments, then bottle tightly in sterilized jars.
Store at room temperature refrigerated or in a cool,
dark place for 2-4 weeks before using.

*This sauce is great on conch (say "konk") and on fresh fish. Rarely
will you find a real Key West Conch who eats his\her seafood without
this flavorful sauce.

Makes: 2 cups

Hot Cocktail Sauce

1 tablespoon prepared horseradish
3 tablespoons ketchup
1 tablespoon chili sauce
3 tablespoons Key Lime juice
Zest* of 1 Key Lime
1 teaspoon Tabasco or other hot sauce
Salt and coarsely ground black pepper to taste

Mix all ingredients together thoroughly. Chill and pour over fresh seafood such as clams, oysters, shrimp, crab meat and Florida lobster, or serve in a separate ramekin.

*Grate the outer peel of 1 Key Lime, but not the white pith (bitter) to enhance the flavor of the sauce.

Makes: About 1 cup

46

Keys' Mustard Sauce

4 cups mayonnaise
1 cup Dijon mustard
3/4 cup Key Lime juice
1 tablespoon Pickapeppa Sauce*
1 tablespoon A-1 Sauce*

Using a whisk or a food processor, blend the mayonnaise with the mustard. Slowly pour in the Key Lime juice. Add the Pickapeppa and A-1 sauce and blend until a light golden brown.

*Available in most supermarkets

Makes: About 5 cups

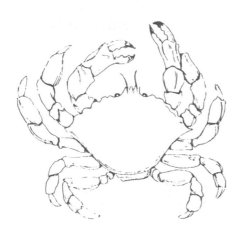

Key Lime Raisin Sauce

1 tablespoon cornstarch
1/2 cup dark brown sugar
1 teaspoon dry mustard
2 tablespoons red wine vinegar
1 tablespoon Key Lime juice
1/2 teaspoon Key Lime or lime zest
1 1/2 cups water
1/3 cup raisins

In a small glass bowl mix the cornstarch together with a small amount of water to form a thin paste.

In a medium size saucepan, mix together the brown sugar, mustard, red wine vinegar, Key Lime juice, Key Lime or lime zest. Add in water, cornstarch mixture and raisins, then cook mixture over low heat, stirring constantly until thick.

Serve over turkey, tongue, fresh pork or baked ham.

Makes: About 1 1/2 cups

Pier House Key Lime Pie

Crust:
1-5 1/2 ounce packet graham crackers, crushed
 (about 1 2/3 cups)
1/4 cup granulated sugar
1/4 cup plus 2 tablespoons butter, melted

Filling:
4 egg yolks
1 14-ounce can sweetened condensed milk
1/2 cup Key Lime juice
1/2 teaspoon cream of tartar

Meringue:
4 egg whites
4 tablespoons superfine sugar

Preheat oven to 325 degrees F.

Separate eggs. Allow at least three hours to prepare ahead.

Prepare the crust ahead by combining all crust ingredients, blending well. Firmly press the cracker mixture evenly over the bottom and sides of a nine inch pie plate. To make it smooth and even, place a smaller pie plate on top of the crumb-filled pie plate. Now, press the smaller pie plate firmly all around the sides and bottom. Bake at 350 degrees F. for six to nine minutes. Cool.

(continued)

To prepare filling, using an electric mixer, beat egg yolks on high speed until thick and light in color. Turn off mixer and add half of the Key Lime juice, and the cream of tartar, then the remaining lime juice. Mix until blended.

Pour into a prepared crust and bake until set, about 10-15 minutes, or until center is firm and dry to touch. Freeze for at least 3 hours before topping with meringue.

To prepare the meringue, heat egg whites in a double boiler with the sugar, stirring frequently to 110 degrees F. Beat on high speed until peaks are formed. Top the frozen pie and return to freezer until serving time. Pie will keep for several days.

Yields: 1 9-inch pie

Joe's Stone Crab Key Lime Pie

Crust:
1 1/4 cups crushed graham crackers
1/3 cup melted butter, or unsalted margarine
1/4 cup granulated sugar

Filling:
2 - 14 ounce cans condensed milk
1 cup Key Lime juice
5 eggs yolks
Zest of 4 Key Limes
1 pint heavy cream, whipped

Preheat oven to 350 F.

To prepare the crust, mix together all of the crust ingredients. Using hands, press to make a crust by evenly spreading to cover the bottom of a 9-inch pan. Insert an 8-inch pan on top of pan to press crumbs together firmly. Bake for about 8 minutes, then cool.

To prepare the filling combine all ingredients and pour into the baked crust. Bake for another 8 minutes. Chill, then freeze for 1 hour before serving.

Serve with huge dollops of whipped cream.

Note: Over 30,000 pies a year are prepared at Joe's Stone Crab on the southern tip of Miami Beach. Each pie is prepared by hand.

Makes: 1 9-inch pie

Classic Key Lime Pie

Crust:
1 1/4 cups graham cracker crumbs
1/4 cup granulated sugar
1/4 cup butter, or margarine

Filling:
1 14-ounce can sweetened condensed milk
4 egg yolks
1/2 cup Key Lime juice,
Freshly whipped cream
1 Key Lime, thinly sliced for garnish

Preheat oven to 325 F. In a medium bowl, mix graham cracker crumbs and sugar together. Melt the butter or margarine and blend well with the cracker crumbs. Press evenly into a 9-inch pie pan. Use an 8-inch pie pan inserted inside the larger pan to press the crumbs into the pan. Bake for 6-8 minutes. Cool for a few minutes.

In another medium size bowl, using an electric mixer, combine the milk and egg yolks at low speed. Slowly add the Key Lime juice. Mix until well blended and mixture is relatively thick. Pour into prepared graham cracker crust and refrigerate overnight. Top with freshly whipped cream and Key Lime slices.

Makes: 1 9-inch pie

Key Lime Rainbow

This recipe was given to me by Chef Beany MacGregor, Executive Chef for the Hard Rock Cafe' in Orlando. This pie appears as a special, but will be featured in another new Rank Worldwide restaurant, Planet Hollywood. Beany uses all fresh juices in this eye-appealing four-layer pie.

Allow at least 8-10 hours for chilling ahead.

Filling:
12 eggs, separated
3 14-ounce cans sweetened condensed milk plus 2 ounces
1/3 cup plus 4 tablespoons Key Lime juice
1/3 cup orange juice
1/3 cup pink grapefruit juice
1/3 cup lemon juice
2 drops red food coloring
2 drops orange food coloring
2 drops yellow food coloring
1 9" deep dish cake round with graham cracker crust

Topping:
1/2 pint heavy whipping cream
1 teaspoon sugar
1 teaspoon Key Lime zest

(continued)

Prepare graham cracker crust according to package directions.

Place three yolks in each of four separate bowls. Set aside each group of 3 egg whites. Place 1 cup of the sweetened condensed milk in each bowl with 1 tablespoon Key Lime juice. Add separately to each of the bowls, and carefully blend the following: 1) 1/3 cup Key Lime juice; 2) 1/3 cup grapefruit juice, 2 drops red food coloring; 3) 1/3 cup orange juice, 2 drops orange food coloring; 4) 1/3 cup lemon juice, 2 drops yellow food coloring. Chill all bowls.

Place 3 of the egg whites in a separate glass mixing bowl and beat at high speed until peaks form. Remove one of the bowls from the refrigerator and stir contents. Fold in egg whites. Pour into cake pan lined with graham cracker crust and place in freezer. When top hardens to touch, repeat the process with the next layer, then the third, and finally, the fourth. Cover and freeze overnight.

Prepare topping with an electric mixer by beating cream to soft peaks. Add sugar and Key Lime zest and blend thoroughly. Serve in large dollops on top of pie.

Makes: 1 9-inch pie

Kooky's Key Lime Pie

1 8-inch graham cracker crust
4 egg yolks
1/2 cup granulated sugar
1/2 cup Key Lime juice
2 cups heavy whipping cream, divided (unwhipped)
1 tablespoon confectioners sugar
1/2 teaspoon vanilla extract

Whisk the egg yolks with the granulated sugar in the top of a double boiler. Simmer over heat for a few minutes, then whisk in the lime juice. Cook for about ten minutes, stirring constantly until the mixture is thick enough to coat a spoon.

Remove from heat, then cover and refrigerate for 1 hour, or until mixture is cool and thick, but not stiff. Whip 1 cup of the cream to the very stiff stage, then fold into the lime filling. Pour into the prepared graham cracker crust and chill thoroughly.

Just before serving, whip the remaining cup of cream to the soft peak stage, then beat in sugar and vanilla. Ladle the whipped cream generously over individual servings of the pie.

Makes: 1 8-inch pie

Cross Creek
Key Lime Pie

1 14-ounce can sweetened condensed milk
Zest* of 6 Key Limes
1/3 cup Key Lime juice
3 egg yolks, beaten
1 1/2 teaspoons overproof (151 proof) white rum
Dash of orange curacao
1 9-inch prepared graham cracker crust
  (see page 49)
1/2 pint heavy cream whipped with 2 tablespoons
confectioner's sugar and 1 tablespoon white rum

Preheat oven to 325 degrees F.

Pour sweetened condensed milk into a large bowl. Add the zest and Key Lime juice. Beat in egg yolks. Add the overproof rum and orange bitters. Pour into a 9-inch prepared graham cracker crust and bake for 8-10 minutes.

Top with fresh whipped cream. Chill until set, about 4 hours.

Note: This recipe was given to me by the Herman family from their landmark Florida restaurant which was called The Yearling after next door neighbor Marjorie Kinnan Rawling's famous story written in Cross Creek, Florida. The recipe has been adjusted to allow the raw egg to cook.

*Grate the outer Key Lime peel, not the white pith (bitter) and add to the mixture.

Makes: 1 9-inch pie

Eggless Key Lime Pie

1 9-inch graham cracker crumb crust, baked
  (see page 49)
2 14-ounce cans sweetened condensed milk
1/2 cup Key Lime juice
Whipped Cream
Zest of Key Lime or lime for garnish

Combine the sweetened condensed milk and the Key Lime juice. Pour mixture into pie shell. Allow pie to cool, then place in freezer until just before serving.

Remove pie from freezer about 1/2 hour before to soften. Top with dollops of fresh whipped cream and grated Key Lime or lime zest.

Makes: 1 9-inch pie

Whipped Chocolate Key Lime Pie

1 15-ounce can sweetened condensed milk
1/2 cup fresh Key Lime juice
8-ounces non-dairy whipped topping
1 9-inch baked graham cracker crust (see page 49)
6-ounces chocolate chips
1 6-ounce milk chocolate bar

    In a medium sized bowl combine the milk and Key Lime juice and beat until thick. Blend in the non-dairy topping and pour into prepared pie crust which has been lined with chocolate chips .

    Refrigerate for at least an hour before serving, or freeze for future use. Shave chocolate bar over top of pie just before serving.

Makes: 1 9-inch pie

Meringue Key Lime Pie

1 9-inch graham cracker shell (see page 49)
1 1/4 cups cold water
3 tablespoons Key Lime juice
1 cup granulated sugar
2 tablespoons cornstarch
3 egg yolks
1 pinch salt
Grated rind of 3 Key Limes
1 tablespoon butter, or margarine
3 egg whites
3 teaspoons granulated sugar
1 9-inch prepared pastry shell

In a double boiler, dissolve the cornstarch in 1/2 cup of cold water. Pour into top part of double boiler. Add the remaining water, the sugar, salt. Break the yolk and stir in briskly to the ingredients. Add the butter or margarine, Key Lime juice, and grated rind. Place the pot over a low heat and stir slowly and constantly until the mixture becomes a thick very heavy cream

Remove from heat. Cool. Add mixture to prepared pastry shell.

Preheat oven to about 500 degrees. To prepare meringue beat egg whites until very stiff. Add sugar, 1 teaspoon at a time. Beat well after adding each teaspoon.

(continued)

To assemble the pie, pour the filling into the baked pastry shell. Distribute it evenly. Pile meringue on top starting from the edge to the center, making certain that the meringue touches the pastry on all sides to prevent it from shrinking. Smooth it with the back of a spoon in a light circular manner. Sift a teaspoon of the sugar over the top of the meringue to give a golden brown crust.

To brown place on top shelf of oven and bake until golden brown, about 2 minutes. Cool. Chill in refrigerator

Makes: 1 9-inch pie

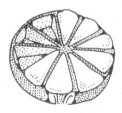

Mile High Key Lime Pie

Crust:
1 1/4 cups graham cracker crumbs
1/4 cup granulated sugar
1/4 cup butter

Filling:
1 14-ounce can sweetened condensed milk
4 egg yolks
1/2 cup Key Lime juice,

Topping:
2 pints heavy cream, whipped
1/4 cup finely chopped walnuts
2 Key Limes, thinly sliced for garnish

Preheat oven to 325 F.
Mix graham cracker crumbs and sugar together. Melt the butter and blend well with the cracker crumbs. Press into a 9-inch pie pan. Use a smaller pie pan to press the crumbs into the pan. Bake for about 6 minutes. Cool.

Using an electric mixer, combine the milk and egg yolks at low speed. Slowly add the Key Lime juice. Mix until well blended and mixture is relatively thick. Pour into prepared graham cracker crust and bake for 8-10 minutes, cool and refrigerate until chilled.

Top mile high with freshly whipped cream, chopped walnuts and chopped Key Lime slices.

Makes: 1 9-inch pie

Captiva Key Lime Pie

This is one of the most famous Key Lime pies in Florida, and certainly on the mystical island of Captiva.

3 egg yolks
3 1/2 ounces Key Lime juice
1 cup (8 ounces) sweetened condensed milk
3 egg whites
1 9" graham cracker pie shell (see page 49)
1 cup heavy cream, whipped
Key Lime slices for garnish

In a large bowl, stir the egg yolks with the Key Lime juice and the sweetened condensed milk. Beat the egg whites until stiff, then gently fold them into the Key Lime mixture, being careful not to deflate it. Pour the mix into the pie shell and freeze until solid. When ready to serve pie, garnish with the whipped cream and slice of lime.

Makes: 1 9-inch pie

No-Bake Cheese Cake

1/2 cup Key Lime juice
1 8-ounce package cream cheese
1 8-ounce container frozen whipped topping, thawed in
  refrigerator
1/3 cup granulated sugar
1 9-inch prepared graham cracker pie crust

Beat cream cheese with a mixer or with a fork until smooth. Gradually add in granulated sugar. Slowly pour in lime juice continuing to blend until smooth, then fold in whipped topping. Blend well. Using a rubber spatula, spoon into graham cracker crust and smooth out. Chill until firm, about 4 hours. Top with additional whipped topping.

Makes: 1 9-inch pie

Low-Cal Key Lime Delight

1 quart low-fat milk
1/8 cup light brown sugar
1 3 - 3/4 package instant vanilla pudding mix
1/4 cup Key Lime juice
2 ice cream scoops lime sherbet
2 ice cream scoops lemon sherbet
Peel of 3 Key Limes
Maraschino cherries and Fresh Mint Sprigs for
  garnish

In the container of a blender, or food processor combine 1/4 cup of milk with the brown sugar. Blend in the remaining milk, then add the pudding mix and blend until very smooth. Add the lime juice and blend a few seconds more. Pour into 4 glasses, adding 1/2 scoop lemon and 1/2 scoop lime to the top of each.
Garnish with lime peel, fresh mint sprigs and maraschino cherries.

Serves: 4

Key Lime Butternut Cookies

1 1/2 teaspoon cornstarch
1 cup all-purpose flour
1/2 teaspoon salt
3/4 teaspoon baking powder
1/2 cup (1 stick) butter
1/2 cup granulated sugar
1 egg yolk, slightly beaten
2 teaspoons Key Lime juice
Grated zest of 3 Key Limes, or zest of 1 lime
1/2 cup chopped walnuts

Preheat oven to 375 degrees F. In a medium size mixing bowl, sift together: the cornstarch, flour, salt and baking powder.

In another mixing bowl, cream the butter with the sugar until
smooth, fluffy and light, then add in the yolk, Key Lime juice and the zest. Slowly add in the sifted ingredients, continuing to mix after each addition. Mix in the walnuts.

Drop by teaspoonsful onto lightly greased cookie sheet, leaving about 2 inches between each cookie. Bake for about 8-10 minutes until edges are lightly browned. Cool.

Makes: About 3 dozen cookies

Pillow Cake

Filling:

3 egg yolks, beaten until thick
1 15-ounce can sweetened condensed milk
Juice of 6 Key Limes
Zest of 6 Key Limes
1 9-inch pie shell, baked

Meringue:

1 cup sugar
1/4 cup water
6 egg whites
Pinch of cream of tartar

Raspberry Puree:

1 pint red raspberries
1/4 cup sugar

To prepare the filling, add the condensed milk to the eggs. Beat on low speed, then add in the Key Lime juice and rind. Chill for a few hours or overnight.

Fill a baked pastry pie shell with the filling. To prepare the meringue, cook the sugar and water until the mixture reaches about 248 degrees on a candy thermometer, or until the mixture forms a soft ball when dropped from a spoon into cold water.

Pillow Cake

Beat egg whites with the tartar until they are stiff. Add the sugar mixture be sure not to pour it on the beaters. Beat on high speed until egg whites are stiff and shiny. Place the meringue in a pastry bag and pile it high onto the pie, or make clouds with dollops of the meringue. Place under a broiler for about 2-3 minutes, being careful to watch. Turn as the meringue browns so it colors evenly.

Puree the raspberries together with the sugar in the container of a blender and process until pureed. Place a few tablespoonfuls on a fancy plate and then add two slices of the Key Lime Pillow.

To assemble, pour some of the puree on each plate. Serve the pillow on top.

From Bryan Homes.

Makes: 1 9-inch cake

Notes:

Aunt Betty's
Key Lime Cake

1 package Duncan Hines lemon supreme cake mix
1/2 cup water
1/2 cup Key Lime juice or lime juice
Zest of 3 Key Limes or 1 regular lime
1 3-ounce package lime jello
1/2 cup vegetable oil
4 eggs, slightly beaten

Frosting:

1/4 pound butter or margarine, softened
1 8-ounce package of cream cheese, softened
1 teaspoon vanilla extract
1 1-pound box confectioners sugar
1-2 tablespoon milk

Using an electric mixer, blend ingredients together until well combined, about 3 minutes. Pour into a greased 9" x 13" x 2" baking pan. Bake for 45 minutes or until a toothpick inserted comes out dry.

To prepare the frosting, use an electric mixer to combine butter, cream cheese, vanilla, confectioners sugar and milk. Blend until smooth and creamy, then add milk to reach the desired consistency. Spread frosting over cake and grate lime over frosting for beautiful tropical effect.

Makes: 1 - 9" x 13" x 2" cake

Bake Cake at 325° F.

Deep Dish Sabayon Tart

4 eggs, slightly beaten
4 yolks
10 ounces granulated sugar
1/2 cup Key Lime juice
5 ounces sweet softened butter

    Combine beaten unsalted eggs, extra yolks, sugar and Key Lime juice and whisk vigorously in a bowl over a double boiler. Cook stirring until thick. Remove from heat, and whisk in the butter.
    Pour into pre-baked pie shell (or tart shell) and
refrigerate 2-3 hours. Serve with a tropical fruit salsa, or tropical sauce.

Makes: 1 8-inch round deep tart.

By Kevin Kopsick, Pastry Chef.

Key Lime Sherbet

2/3 cup granulated sugar
1 teaspoon gelatin
Juice of 18 Key Limes
2 egg whites, beaten stiff
1/8 teaspoon salt
1 1/2 cups water

Combine the sugar and water, stirring as the water boils and the sugar dissolves. Simmer for about 10 minutes. Soften the gelatin by adding a small amount of water, then add. Stir until it is completely dissolved. Chill.

Add the Key Lime juice and pour into an ice tray. Freeze until mixture is about half frozen, then fold in the salt and egg whites which have been beaten until stiff. Replace in the tray. Place in freezer. When mixture becomes mushy, remove and stir again. Return to freezer. Serve when mixture becomes completely frozen.

Serves: 4

Citrus Sorbet

1 cup water
1/2 cup superfine sugar
Juice of 1 lemon
Grated rind of 1 lemon
Juice of 3 Key Limes
Grated rind of 3 Key Limes
1 egg white at room temperature
2 tablespoons Tia Maria liqueur

Dissolve the sugar in water over a low heat. Boil for 2 minutes. Remove from heat, add the lemon and Key Lime rinds and cover for about 10 minutes.

When cooled, add the lemon and Key Lime juice and pour into a shallow freezer container. Freeze for about 2 hours or until thick and soft.

With an electric mixer, whisk egg white until stiff. Turn the mixture into a bowl. Fold in the egg white and Tia Maria and return to container. Freeze until firm.

Serves: 4

Frozen Whipped Delight

3 eggs, separated
1/2 cup sugar
1 cup heavy whipping cream
1/2 cup superfine sugar
1 teaspoon Key Lime peel
1/3 cup Key Lime juice
1 9-inch graham pie shell

In the top of a double boiler beat the egg yolks until light colored and thick. Gradually add the 1/2 cup sugar and the Key Lime juice. Heat for about 5 minutes over simmering water, stirring often. Set aside to cool.

Whip the cream with the superfine sugar in a chilled bowl with chilled beaters. In a separate bowl, beat the egg whites at high speed until stiff, but not dry. Gently fold the beaten egg whites and whipped cream into lime mixture. Stir in the grated peel. Spoon into graham cracker crust. Freeze until firm.

Makes 1 9-inch pie

Key West Slices

1 cup butter or margarine
2 cups all-purpose flour
1 cup confectioners sugar

4 eggs, beaten
2 cups granulated sugar
1 teaspoon baking powder
1/4 cup Key Lime juice
1 teaspoon Key Lime or lime zest
Pinch of salt

Preheat oven to 350 degrees F.

Cream together the butter, flour and sugar until smooth and then press into a 9" x 12" x 2" baking pan so that crust is around sides of pan. Bake for 15 - 20 minutes until crust is lightly browned.

In a separate bowl mix together the eggs, sugar, baking powder, Key Lime juice and zest. Add in a pinch of salt and combine well. Pour mixture on top of hot crust and bake for 20-25 minutes until done. Sift confectioners sugar over top while still warm. Cut into slices or small squares and serve hot or cold.

Serves: 6-8

Miami Key Lime Spiced Mangoes

3 1/2 cups mangoes
1 cup granulated sugar
3/4 cup apple cider vinegar
2 tablespoons Key Lime juice
Zest of 3 Key Limes, or 1 lime
1 teaspoon cloves
1 teaspoon whole allspice
2 sticks cinnamon

Add sugar, vinegar, Key Lime juice, cloves, allspice and cinnamon sticks to a large saucepan. Combine well. Add in mangoes. Cook mixture on high heat for 5 minutes, but be careful not to burn, then allow to simmer for another 10 minutes. Remove from heat, allow to cool. Chill overnight, or at least 8 hours.
Serve alone or over vanilla ice cream.

Serves: 6-8

Key Lime Bread

2/3 cup butter or margarine
2 cups granulated sugar
4 eggs, slightly beaten
3 tablespoons Key Lime juice
Zest of 3 Key Limes or Limes (About 2
tablespoons)
1 teaspoon vanilla extract
3 cups all-purpose flour
2 1/2 teaspoons baking powder
1 teaspoon salt
1 cup milk
1 cup chopped walnuts

Glaze:

3 tablespoons Key Lime juice
2/3 cups granulated sugar

Prepare two loaf pans by greasing well with
margarine or other oil. Preheat oven to 350 degrees
Fahrenheit.
Cream butter or margarine and sugar. Add in
the eggs and beat together well. Pour in the Key
Lime juice, zest and vanilla extract and combine
well. Set aside.

(continued)

In a separate bowl combine the flour, baking powder and salt. Add a little of the milk into the dry mixture, then a little of the creamed mixture alternately until all ingredients are combined, then add in walnuts and mix together gently until mixture forms a nice batter.

Divide into the two loaf pans and bake for 50 to 60 minutes until cakes are firm and nicely browned.

Mix together 3 tablespoons Key Lime juice and the sugar. Spoon mixture over the bread after they are baked. Cool for 15 minutes, then remove from loaf pans. Wrap. Store for about 24 hours, then slice. The bread freezes well.

Makes: 2 loaf pans Key Lime bread.

Our sincere thanks to all of the restaurant owners and managers featured in this book for sharing their favorite recipes with us, without whom this book would not have been possible.